BEST OF
DERVISH

ISBN 0-634-09882-9

7777 W. BLUEMOUND RD. P.O. BOX 13819 MILWAUKEE, WI 53213

Visit Hal Leonard Online at
www.halleonard.com

WHO'S WHO IN DERVISH

CATHY JORDAN
(Vocals, Bodhran & Bones)

Cathy is a native of Scramogue, Co. Roscommon, now living in Sligo. Her love for traditional singing was instilled at an early age, especially by her father. Cathy began singing publicly at all kinds of Feiseanna and concerts as a child. In later years, she took to performing a wide range of material as a solo performer in the midlands. She joined Dervish in 1991 and is now regarded as one of the finest traditional singers in Ireland today.

SHANE MITCHELL
(Accordion)

Shane Mitchell is a Sligo native, and began playing at a very early age. Shane was born into a musical family and he performed at many competitions, both as a solo performer and alongside Dervish band-mate, Liam Kelly, as a duo. Shane learned his craft from noted Sligo accordion player Alfie Joe Dineen. Shane and Liam Kelly formed a very successful traditional group called Poitin, while still both teenagers at school, and as Poitin they appeared on several radio and television programs, and won many competitions. The tight interplay between accordion and flute that stems from this longstanding musical friendship is at the core of the Dervish sound.

LIAM KELLY
(Flute)

Liam Kelly is also a native of Sligo, and began playing at a very young age. Liam comes from musical families, and grew up performing at competitions all over the country, both as a soloist, and as part of a duet with accordionist Shane Mitchell. Liam started his musical career on accordion, but later switched to whistle, and then to flute, learning from local player Carmel Gunning. While still a teenager at school, Liam formed a very successful traditional group called Poitin along with Dervish accordion player Shane Mitchell. They appeared on several television and radio programs, and won many competitions. The tight and intuitive interplay between the flute and accordion are at the core of the Dervish sound, and stem from this long-standing musical friendship.

BRIAN McDONAGH
(*Mandola, Mandolin*)

Brian is an ex-founder of the traditional group Oisin, which had extensive success in the 1970s. Originally from Dublin, Brian moved to Sligo in the '80s after leaving Oisin. As the oldest member of Dervish, he has a great deal of experience touring and performing on the international circuit. He is also an established painter in Ireland, and has many exhibitions, both at home and on the continent.

MICHAEL HOLMES
(*Bouzouki*)

Michael is a native of Sligo and also an ex-member and songwriter of the band Who Says What. His musical background was mostly in the folk and rock genre, but he spent many years playing formally and informally in traditional music. He started playing guitar in his early teens, but later switched to bouzouki. He and fellow member Liam Kelly have co-written several pieces of music, one of which has recently been recorded by Scottish group Capercaille.

TOM MORROW
(*Fiddle*)

Tom is the newest member of Dervish, joining the group in Oct. '98, and is also the youngest band member. Tom is a native of Carrigallen in Co. Leitrim and is the eldest of a musical family including brothers John (banjo), Rob (accordion), and Andy (fiddle). He began playing music at an early age with Tommy Maguire, a native of Glenfarne, Co. Leitrim. During his younger years, he played extensively with a wide range of musicians around Leitrim and Cavan, including Paddy McDermott's Cornafean Group and Antoin McGabhann.

Tom has won numerous awards including the All Ireland Senior Fiddle championship. He has also guested on numerous albums, including recent releases: John Wynne's *With Each Breath*, Galician piper Pepe Vaamonde's *Aviouga*, Eamonn Coyne's *Through the Round Window* and singer Mary McPartland's *The Holland Handkerchief*.

CONTENTS

Ar Éirinn Ní Neosfainn Cé Hí

(For Ireland I Won't Tell Her Name)

Words and Music by Michael Holmes, Cathy Jordan, Liam Kelly,
Shane McAleer, Brian McDonagh and Shane Mitchell

This song seems to bear a similarity to the "Aisling" or "vision poem" style and features some wonderful lyrical verses. Although the air is well known, the song itself is rarely heard. The words are a declaration of the love this poor man has for the daughter of a wealthy family, and his readiness to perform great feats to win her favour. The difference in station is what causes the man to keep her name a secret, but he vows that when they are married and living in "sweet unity" it's then "that her name will be known."

Cathy heard this version of the song from the great old singer, Con Graney. A longer version can be found in Tom Munnelly's tribute to Tom Lenihan – "The Mount Callan Garland."

And the birds ___ sweet - ly sing on ___ each ___ tree

O ___ me dar - ling ___ they're ___ tun - ing their notes

Is ___ ar ___ Éir - inn ___ ní neos - fainn ___ cé hí.

Additional Lyrics

Like a sick man that longs for the dawn
I do long for the light of her smile
And I pray for my own cailín bán
While I'm waiting for her by the stile
O I'd climb all the hills of this land
And I'd swim all the depths of the sea
To get one kiss from her lily-white hand
Is ar Éirinn ní neosfainn cé hí.

I have toiled sore those years of my life
Through storm, through sunshine and rain
And I surely would venture my life
For to shield her one moment from pain
For she being my comfort in life
Though my comfort and joy she may be
She's my own she is my promised wife
Is ar Éirinn ní neosfainn cé hí.

O but when I will call her my own
And it's married we both then will be
Like the King and the Queen on their throne
We'll be living in sweet unity
O it's then I'll have a home of my own
And I'll rear up a nice family
O it's then that her name will be known
But for Ireland I won't tell her name.

The Banks of Sweet Viledee

Words and Music by Michael Holmes, Cathy Jordan, Liam Kelly, Brian McDonagh, Shane Mitchell, Tom Morrow and Séamus O'Dowd

Cathy spent a memorable afternoon with the late Frank Browne from Ballinagare, Co. Roscommon, one of the few collectors from that county. She was introduced to him by Baribre Ní Fhloinn, who was a great friend to him for many years. He gave his time generously, and on that day, Cathy collected many songs from Frank, two of which appear on our album MIDSUMMER'S NIGHT.

He was the sole collector of this version of the song, while other versions are titled: "The House Carpenter," "James Harris" and "The Demon Lover." The location of the "Viledee" is unknown but it may be an Anglicised corruption of an Irish place name.

Frank died in early 1998 and his passing is a great loss to traditional Irish music. We dedicate this song to Frank's memory.

tons of gold ___ I have re - fused ___ And it's all for the love of

you, my ___ love All for the love of you ___

Additional Lyrics

Well, if you could have married a great king's daughter
You have yourself to blame
Well, I have married my house-carpenter
And I think he's a nice young man
Well, if you do leave you house-carpenter
And come along with me
I'll take you to where the grass grows green
On the banks of the Sweet Viledee, my love
Banks of the Sweet Viledee

If I was to leave my house-carpenter
And go along with thee
What have you there to support me with
And keep me from slavery?
Well, I have six ships now sailing out
And seven more on sea
Three hundred and ten all jolly sailsmen
All to wait on thee, my love
All for to wait on thee

She dressed her baby all neat and clean
And gave him kisses three
Saying, "Stay, stay here, my darling baby boy
With you father for company"
She dressed herself in a suit of red
And her maiden waist was green
And every town they passed by
They took her to be some queen, my love
Took her to be some queen

They were not two days out at sea
And I'm sure they were not three
When this fair maid began to weep
And she wept most bitterly
My curse, my curse, and all sailsmen
Who brought me out on sea
And deprived me of my house-carpenter
On the banks of the Sweet Viledee, my love
Banks of the Sweet Viledee

They were not three days out at sea
And I'm sure they were not four
When this fair maid disappeared from the deck
And she sank to rise no more, my love
Sank to rise no more

Bellaghy Fair

Words and Music by Michael Holmes, Cathy Jordan, Liam Kelly,
Shane McAleer, Brian McDonagh and Shane Mitchell

This northern song was given to us by our good friend, Seamus O'Kane from Dungiven,
Co. Derry. Seamus is also a master Bodhran maker and makes all of Cathy's drums.

I went to the fair of Bell-ag-hy, I bought a wee swag of a pig,_____ I gath-ered it up in my arms _ and danced the swag-ger-ing jig. _____ And it's high to the top of the heath-er, and high to the but of the sprig, _____ and high to the bon-nie wee las-sie who danced _ the swag-ger-ing jig.

Additional Lyrics

As I went to the fair of Bellaghy,
I bought a wee slip of a pig,
And being down by the poor house,
I whistled the swaggering jig.
And it's high to the cups and the saucers,
And high to the butter and bread,
And high to the bonnie wee lassie
Who danced the swaggering jig.

I being down by the poor house,
I whistled so loud and so shrill,
I made all the fairies to tremble
That lived around Corcoran's hill.
And it's high to the top of the heather
And high to the but of the sprig,
And high to the bonnie wee lassie
Who danced the swaggering jig.

Cailin Rua

Words and Music by Michael Holmes, Cathy Jordan, Liam Kelly,
Shane McAleer, Brian McDonagh and Shane Mitchell

The words of this song we found in a collection of broadside ballads published by the Cuala Press.
It tells the story of an extraordinary meeting between a well-read gentleman and a rural maid.
He endeavours to impress her by comparing her to the beautiful Goddesses of Greek mythology. She tells him to get lost!

A lot of songs of this "Greek meets Gael" style were written in borrowed "bearla" (English) by hedge
school masters in order to demonstrate their fluency and knowledge.

This song is forever associated with the late great singer and song collector, Paddy Tunney.

As I roved out on a sum-mer's morn - ing, a-spe-cul-at - ing most cu-rious - ly,_____ To my sur-
prise I there e - spied_____ a charm-ing fair_____ one ap-proach-ing me,_____ I stood a-
while in deep med-i-ta - tion con-tem-plat-ing what I should do,_____ 'Til at length
cruit - ing all my_sen - sa - tions I thus ac - cost - ed the Cai-lin Rua.

Additional Lyrics

"Are you Aurora or the Goddess Flora, Artemidora or Venus bright,
Or Helen fair beyond compare that Paris stole from the Grecian sight?
O fairest maiden you have unslaved me, I'm captivated in Cupid's clew,
Your golden saying are infatuations that have enslaved me, a Cailin Rua."

"Kind sir be aisy (easy) and do not tease me with your false praises so jestingly.
Your dissimulations and invocations are vaunting praises alluring me.
I am not Aurora or the Goddess Flora, but a rural maiden to all men's view,
Who's here condoling my situation, my appellation the Cailin Rua."

"Oh were I Hector, that noble victor who died a victim of Grecian skill,
Or were I Paris whose deeds are various, an ar bitrator on Ida's hill,
I'd rage through Asia like Abyssinia, Pennsylvania seeking you
The burning raygions (regions) like sage Orpheus to see your face my sweet Cailin Rua."

Boots of Spanish Leather

Words and Music by Bob Dylan

Cathy was introduced to this song by Fran Hegarty, a long-time friend of Dervish. She chose to sing it for a birthday commemoration held in Dublin to celebrate Bob Dylan's 60th birthday, and later introduced it to the band.

Just — car - ry your - self back _____ to me _____ un - spoiled _____

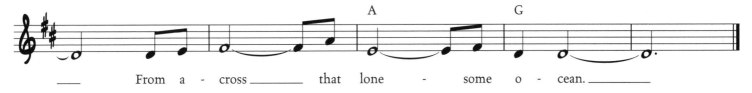

_____ From a - cross _____ that lone - some o - cean. _____

Additional Lyrics

There's nothin' you can send me, my own true love
There's nothin' I wish to be ownin'
Just carry yourself back to me unspoiled
From across that lonesome ocean.

Oh, but I just thought you might want something fine
Made of silver or of golden
Either from the mountains of Madrid
Or from the coast of Barcelona?

Oh, but if I had the stars from the darkest night
And the diamonds from the deepest ocean
I'd forsake them all for your sweet kiss
For that's all I'm wishin' to be ownin'.

That I might be gone a long time
And it's only that I'm askin'
Is there something I can send you to remember me by
To make your time more easy passin'?

Oh, how can, how can you ask me again
It only brings me sorrow
The same thing I want from you today
I would want again tomorrow.

I got a letter on a lonesome day
It was from his ship a-sailin'
Saying I don't know when I'll be comin' back again
It depends on how I'm feelin'.

Well, if you, my love, must think that way
I'm sure your mind is roamin'
I'm sure your thoughts are not with me
But with the country to where you're goin'.

So take heed, take heed of the western wind
Take heed of the stormy weather
And yes, there's something you can send back to me
Spanish boots of Spanish leather.

The Cocks Are Crowing

Words and Music by Michael Holmes, Cathy Jordan, Liam Kelly, Brian McDonagh, Shane Mitchell, Tom Morrow and Séamus O'Dowd

Hugh Shields recorded a version of this song from the County Down singer Eddie Butcher in 1966.
In his book ADAM IN PARADISE, 1969, Shields says of this song:

"A young man taps at a girl's window before daybreak and pleads with her to elope with him.... Their dialogue at the window and
their parting are full of exquisite poetry which puts this English song among the best of Eddie's repertory.... the song
seems relatively rare in Ireland and Eddie's version of it is quite unique." Cathy first heard this sung by the Voice Squad.

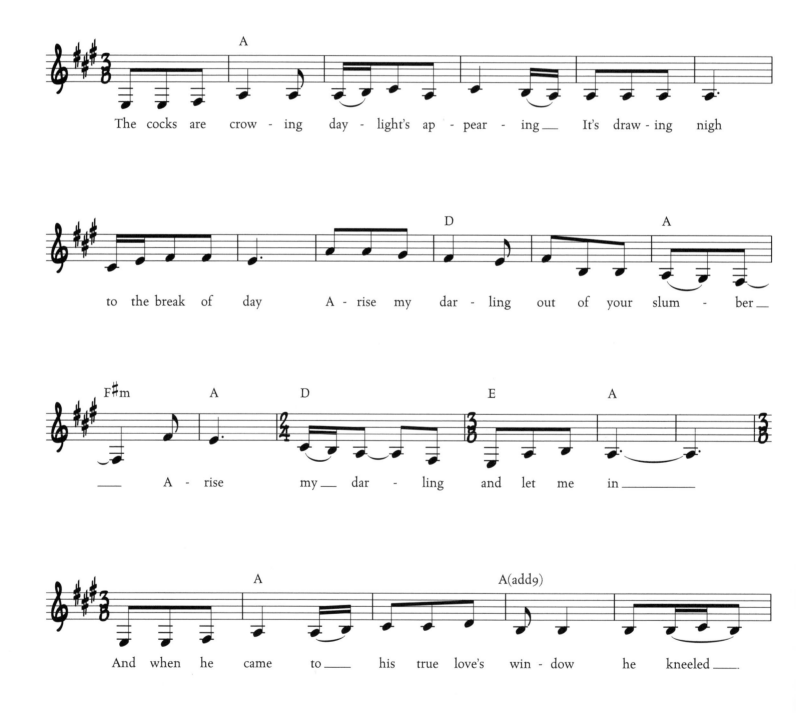

low __ down up-on a __ stone And through the win - dow he whis-pered

soft - ly, __ "A - rise my __ dar - ling and let me in" _____

Additional Lyrics

And when he came to his true love's window
He kneeled low down upon a stone
And through the window he whispered softly
"Arise my darling and let me in"

"Well who is that that is at my window
And who is that that gives me no rest"
"Tis I, tis I a poor wounded lover
Who fain would speak with you love awhile"

"Then go away love and ask your daddy
If he would have you my bride to be
And if he says no then return and tell me
For this is the last time I will trouble thee"

"Oh my dada is in his bed chamber
He's fast asleep on his bed of ease
But in his pocket there lies a letter
Which reads far love on to your disgrace"

"Oh what disgrace can he do unto me
A faithful husband to you I'll be
And what other neighbours have round their houses
The same my darling you would have with me"

"Then go away love and ask your mammy
If she would have you my bride to be
But if she says no then return and tell me
For this is the last time I will trouble thee"

"Oh my mama she's an old aged woman
And scarce can hear love one word I say
But she'd have you go love and court some other
For I'm not a fitting girl your bride to be"

"I'll go away but I'll court no other
My heart is linked all on your charms
I'd have you go love and leave your mammy
For you're only fit to lie in your love's arms"

"I'll go away unto the wild mountains
Where I'll see nothing but the wild deer
And I'll eat nothing but the wild herbs sure
I'll drink nothing but my true love's tears"

"If the Kellybawn it were mine in the chorus
And the green fields they were mine and wide
If my pen was made of the tempered steel sure
My true love's praises I could never write"

Eileen McMahon

Words and Music by Michael Holmes, Cathy Jordan, Liam Kelly, Shane McAleer, Brian McDonagh and Shane Mitchell

Again, an example of an Aisling. The beautiful girl appears in a dream and laments the plight of old Ireland. Cathy learned this song from her father, Pat Joe, who died in January 1994. It was his party piece.

Last night as I lay on my pil-low __ A vi-sion ap-peared in my __ view of a ship sail-ing o-ver the o-cean And the wind it tre-men-dous-ly blew.

* chords are optional

Additional Lyrics

On the deck stood a handsome young lady
With features I ne'er saw before
And she sighed for the wrongs of her country
Saying I'm banished from Erin's green shore.

In thought I approached this young lady
And asked her the cause of her woe
She said I'm only an exile from Erin
The land where the green shamrocks grow.

For the want of employment in Erin
I am forced as an exile to roam
Far away from my home in Killarney
And the beautiful spot at the Doe.

Far away from each mountain and valley
From the punch bowl to the gap of Dunlow
All around the green shores of sweet Mireress
Where in childhood I once used to roam.

My name it is Eileen McMahon
My age it is scarcely eighteen
I thank you kind sir for your kindness
You don't know how lonely I have been.

It was then I awoke from my slumber
I looked for my Eileen to see
There was only the face of my mother
As she gazed with a fond smile on me.

For the ship on the ocean had vanished
But in fancy I see her once more
My beautiful Eileen McMahon
The pride of old Erin's green shore.

Érin Grá Mo Chroí
(Ireland My Heart's Love)

Words and Music by Michael Holmes, Cathy Jordan, Liam Kelly,
Brian McDonagh, Shane Mitchell, Tom Morrow and Séamus O'Dowd

We first heard this song sung by Seamus O'Donnell from Aclare, Co. Sligo, when we stopped into Matt Molloy's
pub one day for a cup of tea. It took seven hours to drink the tea, but the song stayed with us since.

Additional Lyrics

'Twas on a cold, cold winter's night with the turf fire burning bright
And the snowflakes fallen on a winter's day
And I been all alone, I sat down on my own
In the dear little isle so far away
(Chorus)

The day that I did part, sure it broke my mother's heart
Will I ever see my dear folks anymore?
Not until my bones are laid in the cold and silent grave
In the dear little isle so far away
(Chorus)

The Fair Haired Boy

By Brendan Graham

*Our good friend Brendan Graham gave this song to us. It is part of the soundtrack Brendan wrote
to compliment his best-selling book THE WHITEST FLOWER published by Harper Collins.
The song is set in the 19th century during the Irish famine, and tells of the sorrow of parting.*

Oh my fair-haired boy, no more I'll see you walk the mead - ows
green; or hear your song run through the fields like yon moun-tain stream your
ship waits on the west-ern shore to bear you o'er from me but
wait I will 'til heav-en's door my fair-haired boy to see

Additional Lyrics

All joy is gone that we once knew
All sorrow newly found
Soon you'll in California be
Or Colorado bound
Let no sad tears now stain your cheek
As we kiss our last goodbye;
Think not upon when we might meet
My love, my fair-haired boy

If not in life we'll be as one
Then, in death, we'll be;
And there will grow two hawthorn trees
Above my love and me.
And they will reach up to the sky
Intertwined be;
And the hawthorn flower will bloom where lie
My fair-haired boy and me

The Fair Maid

Words and Music by Michael Holmes, Cathy Jordan, Liam Kelly, Shane McAleer, Brian McDonagh and Shane Mitchell

We got this song from the singing of Triona ni Domhnaill. The theme of the lady going to sea in sailors' clothes must have been a popular one considering the number of songs which feature it.

When I was a fair maid a - bout sev - en - teen I list - ed in the na - vy, for to serve the Queen. I list - ed in the na - vy, a sai - lor lad to stand, for to hear the can - nons rat - tle and the mu - sic so grand. The mu - sic so grand, the mu - sic so grand, for to hear the can - nons rat - tling and the mu - sic so grand.

Additional Lyrics

The officer who listed me was a tall and handsome man,
He said, "You'll make a sailor lad, so come along, my man."
My waist being tall and slender, my fingers long and thin,
And the very soon they learned me, I soon exceeded them.
I soon exceeded them, I soon exceeded them
And the very soon they learned me I soon exceeded them.

They sent me to my bed they sent me to my bunk,
To lie with the sailor I never was afraid,
But taking off my blue coat, sure it often made me smile,
For to think I was a sailor and a maiden all the while.
A maiden all the while, A maiden all the while…
For to think I was a sailor and a maiden all the while…

They sent me up to London, for to guard the Tower,
And I'm sure I might be there until my very dying hour,
But a lady fell in love with me, I told her I was a maid
She went unto the captain and my secret she betrayed.
My secret she betrayed, My secret she betrayed
She went unto the captain and my secret she betrayed.

Well the captain, he stepped up to me and he asked if
    this was so.
I dare not, I dare not, I dare not say no.
" 'Tis a pity we should lose you, such a sailor lad you made,
It's a pity we should lose you, such a handsome young maid.
A handsome young maid, A handsome young maid
It's a pity we should lose you such a handsome young maid."

So fare thee well, my captain, you've been so kind to me,
And likewise, my shipmates, I'm sorry to part with thee
But if ever the navy needs a lad, a sailor I'll remain,
I'll put on me cap and feathers and I'll run the rigging again.
I'll run the rigging again, I'll run the rigging again,
I'll put on me cap and feathers and I'll run the rigging again.

Hills of Greenmore

Words and Music by Michael Holmes, Cathy Jordan, Liam Kelly, Shane McAleer, Brian McDonagh and Shane Mitchell

A song that falls into the hunting category concerning the pursuit of a witch hare with magic powers. In recent years Cathy actually met the hunters' grandchildren who still live in Keady. This song was very popular in the early 1970s through the singing of Al O'Donnell, but has not been heard much in recent years. Other versions include "The Creggan White Hare" and "The Greanmore Hare."

On _____ a fine sum - mer's morn - ing our ___ horns we did blow To the green fields ___ round Tai - seal where the hunts - men did go ___ ___ For to meet the bold sports - men from a - round Kea - dy town ___ _____ for ___ none loves sport bet - ter than the boys from mead - ow. ___

Additional Lyrics

And when we arrived they were all standing there
We set off for the fields, boys, in search of a hare
We didn't get far till someone gave the cheer
Over high hills and valleys the sweet puss did steer.

As we flew o'er the hills, 'twas a beautiful sight
There was dogs black and yellow, there was dogs black and white
Now she took the black bank for to try them once more
Oh it was her last look o'er the Hills of Greenmore.

"No more o'er the green fields of Keady I'll roam
To trip through the fields, boys, in sport and in fun
Or hear the long horn that your toner does play
Or go home to my den by the clear light of day."

You may blame ol' Mac Mahon for killing the hare
For he's at his ol' capers this many's a year
On Saturday and Sunday he never gives o'er
With a pack of strange dogs round the Hills of Greenmore.

I Courted a Wee Girl

Words and Music by Michael Holmes, Cathy Jordan, Liam Kelly, Shane McAleer, Brian McDonagh and Shane Mitchell

This was the first song we heard from the singing of the late Mrs. Sarah Makem from Keady, County Armagh.
We incorporated a piece of music into the song called "Josefin's Waltz" which we got from the Swedish group Väsen.
The idea of blending the two together came about in a dressing room in Stockholm!

The story of the man being rejected by the woman in favour of a richer husband is very similar to
another song – "The Lambs on the Green Hills," in Colm O'Lochlainn's book Irish Street Ballads.

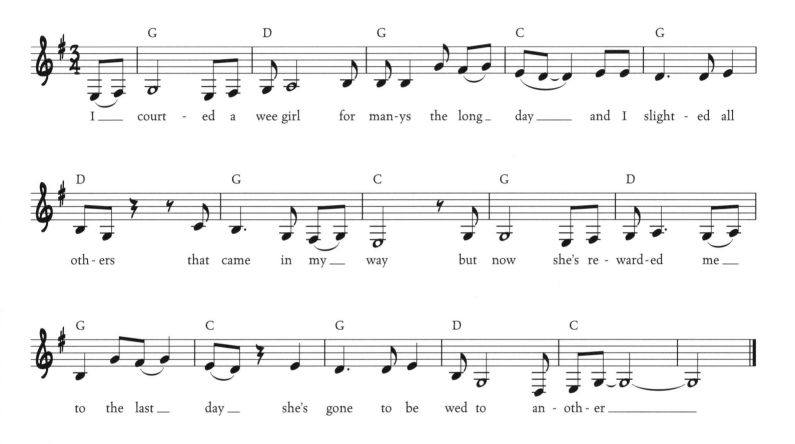

Additional Lyrics

The bride and bride's party to church they did go
The bride she rode foremost she put the best show
And I followed after with a heart full of woe
To see my love wed to another

The bride and bride's party in church they did stand
Gold rings on their fingers, a love by the hand
And the man that she's wed to has houses and land
He may have her since I couldn't gain her

The next time I saw her she was seated down neat
I sat down beside her not a bite could I eat
For I thought my love's company far better than meat
Since love was the cause of my ruin

The last time I saw her she was all dressed in white
And the more I gazed on her she dazzled my sight
I lifted my hat and I bade her goodnight
Here's adieu to all false-hearted lovers

I courted that wee girl for manys the long day
And I slighted all others that came in my way
And now she's rewarded me too the last day
She is gone to be wed to another

So dig me a grave and dig it down deep
And strew it all over with primrose so sweet
And lay me down easy no more for to weep
Since love was the cause of my ruin

The Lag's Song

Words and Music by Ewan MacColl

This song was written by Ewan McColl in 1956. It was used as the musical theme for IN PRISON, a documentary film made in Strangeways Prison, Manchester, by the English film-maker, Dennis Mitchell. Séamus has known the song for several years, having first come across it on the Dubliners album DUBLINERS TOGETHER AGAIN, 1979.

When I was a young man Some-times I'd won-der What hap-pened to time as it passed Then one day I found out That time just lands in pri-son And there it is held fast

Additional Lyrics

When I was a young man
I used to go courting
Underneath the moon and stars
The moon is still shining
But the dreams they are all broken
On these hard iron bars

Look out of the window
Over the rooftops
Over the wall, up to the sky
Just one flying leap and you
Could make your getaway
If only you could fly

The prison is sleeping
The nightwatch is keeping
His watch over seven hundred men
And behind every cell door
A sleeping lad lies dreaming
Oh, to be free again

Repeat 1st verse

Molly and Johnny

Words and Music by Michael Holmes, Cathy Jordan, Liam Kelly,
Shane McAleer, Brian McDonagh and Shane Mitchell

A song we heard from the singing of the late Joe Holmes from the Co. Antrim. The theme of the young woman donning the uniform and following her loved one to sea is a common one. In this version, the man lacks enthusiasm for the idea and does his best to dissuade the lady by painting a bleak picture of life at sea.

Additional Lyrics

Said Molly to Johnny Oh, I will mourn for you
And I will be grieved at your going away
For you know very well that your absence does grieve me
I'm afraid you might die in some strange country

I'll dress myself up like a neat little sea boy
Amidst all life's dangers I will stand your friend
Through the winds that lie lofty and high winds that are blowing
My dear I'd be with you to plough the rough main

Your delicate fingers our ropes could not handle
Your lily-white feet love our decks could not stand
Nor the cold nights of winter you ne'er could endure them
So stay at home darling to the seas do not go

Lone Shanakyle

Words and Music by Michael Holmes, Cathy Jordan, Liam Kelly,
Shane McAleer, Brian McDonagh and Shane Mitchell

At the time of recording, we had only a little information concerning the origins of this song. We believed it was written in exile sometime in the 19th century. Only this year (2004) while performing at the Mrs. Crotty festival in Kilrush, Co. Clare, we were delighted to meet (and perform the song for) the descendents of the composer, Thomas Madigan (1797-1881). Thomas was a scholar poet from Carnacalla, Kilrush, Co. Clare. It's believed he wrote the song sometime in the 1860s.

Shanakyle (in Irish SeanaChill - the old church) is the site of a famine graveyard outside Kilrush, Co. Clare.

The melody is from a very old air entitled "An Paistín Fionn" (The Fairhaired Boy). We have wondered long and hard about this song's combination of a bright tune with powerful, sad, and sometimes frightening lyrics.

head-lands ap-pear - ing___ Cloud-ed in silv-'ry spray,___ thrash-ing through

heav-en's bright___ ray For the glo-ry and pride of poor___ E - rin_____

Additional Lyrics

Sweet, sweet Inis Cathaigh that's sacred and blessed
A fit place for a saint or a warrior's rest
O God that a bear should be best of his brood
Who now bites your beauty my Erin
(Chorus)

How dearly I long for to wander once more
To the old ones I left round my own cabin door
My blessings I gave ten thousand times o'er
With a prayer and a tear for poor Erin
(Chorus)

Sad, sad is my fate in weary exile
Dark, dark are the night clouds round lone Shanakyle
Your murdered sleep silently pile upon pile
In the coffinless graves of poor Erin
(Chorus)

I am watching and praying through the length of the night
For the grey dawn of freedom my signal to fight
My rifle is ready my sabre is bright
For to strike once again for poor Erin
(Chorus)

Peata Beag
(Little Pet)

Words and Music by Michael Holmes, Cathy Jordan, Liam Kelly, Shane McAleer, Brian McDonagh and Shane Mitchell

A "dandling" or childrens' song which a mother would sing to her child while rocking them on her knee.
The lyrics are very simple, but they have a certain charm all the same.

Brendan Breathnach in his book FOLK MUSIC AND DANCES OF IRELAND *believes the Normans introduced this type of song into Ireland in the 12th century. The "Carol," as it was known then, was a type of love song dance comprised of three repeated lines with a concluding fourth. A leader would sing the first three lines in the round dance with everyone joining on the last line. We got "Peata Beag" from Brian, who used to perform it with the band Oisin. The song is introduced and resolved with a piping jig called variously "Coppers and Brass," and "The Humours of Ennistymon."*

Is tru-a gan pea-ta'n mhaoir a-gam, Is trua gan pea-ta'n mhoair a-gam, Is tru-a gan pea-ta'n mhaoir a-gam, 'Sna caoi-righ bea-ga bá-na. Is ó gairm gairm ____ thú Is grá mo chroí gan chei-lig thú,_ Is ó gairm gairm ____ thú 'S'tú pea-ta beag_ do mhá-thair ____

Additional Lyrics

Is trua gan maoilín bhán agam	Is trua gan bólacht bainne agam	Is trua gan gabhirín bhuí agam
Is trua gan maoilín bhán agam	Is trua gan bólacht bainne agam	Is trua gan gabhirín bhuí agam
Is trua gan maoilín bhán agam	Is trua gan bólacht bainne agam	Is trua gan gabhirín bhuí agam
Is failte ó mo ghrá geal	Is Cáitín O' na mháthair?	Is thabharfainn do mo stór é.
Is ó gairm gairm thú...	Is ó gairm gairm thú...	Is ó gairm gairm thú...

Translation

It's a pity I haven't the Steward's pet (3Xs)
And a little white sheep

Chorus:
And O, I call you, I call you
you are my heart's love without deceit
And O, I call you, I call you
And you are your mother's little pet

It's a pity I haven't a bright little treasure (3Xs)
And a welcome from my true love

It's a pity I haven't a milking herd (3Xs)
And a kitten from my mother

It's a pity I haven't a little yellow goat (3Xs)
I would give it to my darling

Peigín Mo Chroí
(Little Peg My Love)
Words and Music by Michael Holmes, Cathy Jordan, Liam Kelly, Shane McAleer, Brian McDonagh and Shane Mitchell

This is a version of a song which can be heard in the west of Ireland. We heard it sung by the late great sean nos singer, Joe Heaney from Carna, Co. Galway. He also had an English song with a similiar tale entitled "Seven Drunken Nights" made famous by the Dubliners. This Irish version is thought to be a condensed extract from a folk tale wherein a farmer is advised to be prudent in all decisions. The song is the humourous story of a man returning home after a long spell away (a drinking spree?) to find a tall, young, bearded man about his house. When told it is his son he has never seen, he replies by saying he has travelled manys the place "but a beard on a child I never saw before."

A Pheg-ín mo cha-ra is a Pheg-ín mo chroí cé hé an fear fa-da tim peall an tí? Oh ahoah, oh hi ho ha oh a ho - ah, Pheg-ín mo chroí _____

Additional Lyrics

A Pheadar mo chara is a Pheader mo chroí
Sin e do mhaicin nach bhfaca tu riamh
curfá:
Oh...etc
Pheadar mo chroi

Shuil mise thoir is shuil mise thiar
is feasóg ar leanabh ní fhaca mé riamh
curfá

A Pheadar mo chara is a Pheadar mo chroí
Eirigh do sheasamh 'gus reitigh greim bia
curfá

A Phegín mo chara is a Phegín mo chroí
níl ins an teach ach aon greim mine buí
curfá

A Pheadar mo chara is a Pheadar mo chroí
in íochtar mo mhála tá cáca min buí
curfá

A Phegín mo chara is a Phegín mo chroí
tá an cáca seo ró fada níl aon chaoí buí
curfá

's a Pheadar mo chara suifimis síos
Na fagfas an baile chomh's mhairfeas mé riamh
curfá

A Phegín mo chara is a Phegín mo chroí
Cé hé an fear fada timpeall an tí?
curfá

Translation

Peg my friend and Peg my heart
who is the long man around the house?

Ohhh...etc. Peg my heart.

Peter my friend and Peter my heart
That is your son you never saw before

I have walked east and I have walked west
but a beard on a child I never saw before

Peter my friend and Peter my heart
stand up and sort out a bite of food

Peg my friend and Peg my heart
there's nothing in the house but one yellow meal cake

Peter my friend and Peter my heart
in the bottom of my bag there is a yellow meal cake

Peg my friend and Peg my heart
This cake is too long there and is in a poor yellow condition?

Seán Bháin
(Fair Sean)

Words and Music by Michael Holmes, Cathy Jordan, Liam Kelly, Brian McDonagh, Shane Mitchell, Tom Morrow and Séamus O'Dowd

*High in Cathy's social calendar is a little festival in Connemara called "Siamsa Choilm De Bhailís."
It was there she heard this song being sung by Colm Seoighe and Mairtín Tom Sheainín. The song tells
about a young woman who invites the handsome Seán to have his evil way with her in "the cock of hay."*

Additional Lyrics

A_Sheáin Bháin, beir orm
'S a Sheáin Bháin, bréag mé
A_Sheáin Bháin, beir orm
Is tabhair sa gcoca féir mé

Shúil mise Sasana
An Fhrainc uilig trí chéile
Is ní fhaca mé aon siobaire
Ba dheise ná do chírín
(Chorus)

Nach deas an baile an baile seo
Nach deas an baile é Maoras
Nach deas an baile chuile baile
Ach Claidhneach glas na bhfaochain
(Chorus)

A Mháire, má tá tú ag scarúint uaim
Mo mhíle slán go deo leat
Nach deas mar chuirfinn fataí dhuit
Níos fearr ná bhainfinn móin dhuit
Nach olc an t-am a d'imigh tú
'S an fómhar ann go díreach
Is gan éinne ar an mbaile seo
Ná bean óg le thú chaoineadh
(Chorus)

Is cuma liom cá rachaidh tú
Is cuma liom cá mbíonn tú
Is cuma liom cá rachaidh tú
Ach thú beith ann san oíche
(Chorus)

A Sheáin Bháin, beir orm
'S a Sheáin Bháin, bréag mé
A Sheáin Bháin, beir orm
Nár phóg tú aréir mé

Translation

Fair-haired Sean, catch me
Fair-haired Sean, lie to me
Fair-haired Sean, catch me
And take me into the cock of hay

It's lovely the way the cock's crest grows
It's lovely the way the hen's crest grows
It's lovely the way the cock's crest grows
For Kathleen Griffin

I walked to England
France all together
And I never saw a crest as nice
As the one on your hen

Isn't this town nice?
Isn't Maoras a nice town?
Isn't every town nice?
Except Clidhnach, green with periwinkles

Mary, if you're leaving me
A thousand farewells
Wouldn't I sow your potatoes well
Even better than I'd cut turf for you

Didn't you go at a bad time
And autumn just here
And no one here
No young woman to cry for you

I don't care where you go
I don't care where you are
I don't care where you go
As long as I have you at night

Fair-haired Sean, catch me
Fair-haired Sean, lie to me
Fair-haired Sean, catch me
Didn't you kiss me last night?

Sheila Nee Iyer

Words and Music by Michael Holmes, Cathy Jordan, Liam Kelly,
Shane McAleer, Brian McDonagh and Shane Mitchell

This song we learned from the singing of Paddy Tunney and is another example of what he calls "Greek meets Gael"
(see also "Cailín Rua"). The original Sile Ni Ghadhra is an 18th century song/poem of the "Aisling" variety (a vision or
dream), where the poet encounters a beautiful woman who usually symbolises Ireland in distress. This particular song is a
little more down to earth and tells of a meeting between a dreamy poetic scholar and a beautiful (but very practical) rural
maiden who has no time to waste listening to a "rhyming rogue." Despite his lyrical, high-minded effusions, she orders
him to "Be off to your speirbhean" (woman of the sky). Apparently, flattery really does get you nowhere...

Additional Lyrics

"Go rhyming rogue let my flocks roam in peace
You won't find amongst them that famed Golden Fleece
The tresses of Helen, that goddess of Greece,
Have hanked round your heart like a doll of desire
Be off to your speirbhean" said Sheila Nee Iyer.

"May the sufferings of Sisyphus fall to my share
And may I the torments of Tantalus bear
To the dark land of Hades let my soul fall an heir
Without linnet in song or a note on the lyre
If ever I prove false to you Sheila Nee Iyer.

"O had I the wealth of the Orient store
Or the gems of Peru or the Mexican Ore
Or the hand of a Midas to mould o'er and o'er
Bright bracelets of gold and of flaming sapphire
I'd robe you in splendour my Sheila Nee Iyer."

Soldier Laddie

Words by Robbie Burns
Arranged by Michael Holmes, Cathy Jordan, Liam Kelly,
Brian McDonagh, Shane Mitchell, Tom Morrow and Séamus O'Dowd

The words of this song were composed by Robert Burns in 1785 as part of his cantata "The Jolly Beggars."
They were not published until after his death. The tune "Sodger Laddie" which Burns indicated as the tune to which
this song was to be sung, may have been a popular tune at the time. Cathy first heard this song from her good friend
Amy O'Hara, who learned it at the Tubbercurry Summer School.

I once was a maid but I can-not tell ___ when ___

___ Still my de-light is in pro-per young men Some ___

one of a troop of dra-goons was my dad-dy No ___ won-der I

fell for a young sol-dier lad-die Sing fol de rol ral de ra

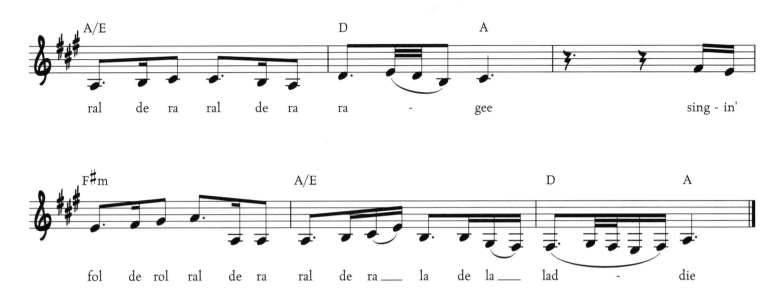

ral de ra ral de ra ra - gee sing - in'

fol de rol ral de ra ral de ra la de la lad - die

Additional Lyrics

The first of my loves was a swaggering blade
To rattle the thundering drum was his trade
His leg was so tight and his cheek was so ruddy
Transported was I with my young soldier laddie
Sing fol...etc

But the Godly old chaplin left him in the lurch
The gun I forsook for the sake of the church
He ventured the soul and I risked the body
'Twas then I proved false to my young soldier laddie
Sing fol...etc

Full soon I grew sick of my sanctified thoughts
To the regiment at large for a husband I sought
From the gilded spitoon to the fife I was ready
And I asked for no more than a young soldier laddie
Sing fol...etc

But the peace it reduced me to beg in despair
Till I met my old laddie at Canningham Fair
His rags regimental they fluttered so gaudy
And my heart did rejoice in my young soldier laddie
Sing fol...etc

Now I have lived for I know not how long
But still I can join in a cup or a song
While with both hands I can hold the glass steady
Here's to you my love my young soldier laddie
Sing fol...etc

An Spailpín Fánach
(The Roving Labourer)
Words and Music by Michael Holmes, Cathy Jordan, Liam Kelly,
Shane McAleer, Brian McDonagh and Shane Mitchell

The life of the travelling labourer who tramped the roads of Ireland seeking work on the farms at harvest time was a hard one. It was back-breaking work, and all for a pittance or just a meal and somewhere to sleep. These labourers were badly treated by the landowners, and the word "spailpín" even became a term of abuse meaning "a lowly or poor character."

This is a great old song of a man whose people fell on hard times through eviction, forcing him to hire himself as a spailpín. He escapes from this miserable existence by joining with the French army to fight overseas. Unfortunately, he ends up "Poor, miserable and alone in these foreign lands" and laments as he remembers what broke his heart and drove him from home.

- fraí an bhfuil - im hír ál ta "Ó

téa - nam chun siúil tá an cúr - sa fa - da" Seo ar siúl an Spail - pín Fá - nach

Additional Lyrics

Im Spailpín Fánach fágadh mise,
Ag seasamh ar mo shláinte,
Ag siúl an drúchta go moch ar maidin.
'S ag bailiú galair ráithe.
Ní fheicfear corrán im' láimh chun bainte,
Súiste ná feac beag ráinne,
Ach bratacha na bhFranncach os cionn
mo leapan
Is píce agam chun sáite

Mo chúig céad slán chun dúiche m'athar
'Gus chun an oileáin ghrámhair
Is chun buachaill na Cúlach os díobh
nár mhiste
In aimsir chasta an ghárda,
Ach anois ó táimse im chadhan
bhocht dhealbh
Imeasc na ndúichi fáin seo
'Sé mo chumha croí mar fuair mé an ghairm,
Bheith riamh im Spailpín Fánach

Is ró-bhreá is cuimhin liom mo dhaoine
bheith sealad
Thiar ag droichead Gháile,
Fé bhuaí, fé chaoraí, fé laoi bheaga gheala
Agus capaill ann le h-áireamh.
Acht b'é toil Chríost é gur cuireadh sinn asta,
'S go ndeaghamhar I leith ár sláinte,
'S gurbh é bhris mo chroí i ngach tír
dá rachainn
"Call here, you Spailpín Fánach."

Translation

Never again will I go to Cashel
Selling and trading my health
Nor to the hiring-fair sitting by the wall
A lounger on the roadside
The bucks of the country coming on their horses
Asking if I'm hired
"Oh, let's go, the journey is long"
Off goes the travelling worker

I was left as an itinerant labourer
Depending on my health
Walking the dew early in the morning
Ccatching all the illnesses going around
You'll not see a hook in my hand for harvesting
A flail or a short spade,
But the flag of France over my bed
And the pike for stabbing

Five hundred farewells to the land of my father
And to the dear island
And to the boys of Cualach because they never
Feared in the troubled times on defence,
But now that I am poor, miserable and alone
In these foreign lands
I'm broken-hearted I got the call to be a travelling labourer

I well remember my people were at one time
Over at the bridge at Gáil
With cattle, with sheep, with little white calves
And plenty of horses
But it was the will of God that we were evicted
And we were left with only our health
And what broke my heart every where I went
"Call here you spalpín fanach."

A Stór Mo Chroí

Words and Music by Michael Holmes, Cathy Jordan, Liam Kelly,
Shane McAleer, Brian McDonagh and Shane Mitchell

A song of immigration composed relatively recently by Brian O'Higgins of Banta (?).
We first heard this beautiful song from Sean Horan, a great old singer at sessions in Sligo town.

A __ Stór Mo Chroí, __ when you're far a - way __ From the home __

__ you'll __ soon __ be leav - ing, And it's man - y a time __

by __ night and day __ your __ heart __ will __ sore - ly be

griev - ing. For the stran - ger's land is rich and __ fair, with rich - es and

treas - ures gol - den You'll __ pine, I __ know, for the long, __ long a - go __

__ And the love that's __ nev - er ol - den.

Additional Lyrics

A Stór Mo Chroí, in the stranger's land
There's plenty of wealth and earnings
Wealth and gems adorn the rich and grand
But there are faces with hunger tearing

Though the road is weary, and hard to tread
And the lights of the city may blind you
You'll turn, a stor, for Erin's shore
And the ones you have left behind you.

A Stór Mo Chroí, when the evening sun
Over mountain and meadow is falling,
Won't you turn away from the throng and listen
And maybe you'll hear me calling.

Though the voice you'll hear is surely mine
For someone's speedy returning
Aroon, aroon, won't you come home soon
To the ones who will always love you.

Willie Lennox

Words and Music by Michael Holmes, Cathy Jordan, Liam Kelly, Shane McAleer, Brian McDonagh and Shane Mitchell

A very sad song concerning the drowning of a young Willie Lennox in Loch Inisholin (Lough Inis O'Lynn – the lake and island of the O'Lynn's). There are many versions of this song which is commonly known as "The Lakes of Coolfin." This version we got from singer Phil Callery, who in turn heard it from the Northern song collector and singer, Len Graham.

It was ear-ly one morn-ing Wil-lie Len-nox a-rose and straight to his cou-sin's bed cham-ber he goes saying "A-rise, love-ly cou-sin and let no one know, 'tis a fine sum-mer's morn-ing to the lakes let us go."

Additional Lyrics

As Willie and his cousin went down the long lane
They met Sargent Henry and Colonel Ronayne
Said the Colonel "Do not enter, do not venture in
For there's deep and false waters in Lough Inisholin."

But Willie being stout-hearted it's in he did go
He swam to an island which was his overthrow
He swam it twice over, was turning around
And in a few minutes Willie Lennox was drowned.

Small boats they were lowered, long lines were let down
And in a few minutes Willie Lennox was found
There was an old woman being there standing by
She ran to his mother and this she did cry:

(This verse is a shorter half verse – first eight bars only)
"Sad news I have for you which grives my heart sore
For your own darling Willie his name is no more."

And as for his true love who mourns night and day
For the loss of her true love who lies cold in the clay
For both morning and evening he did her salute
With the pink and red roses and all garden fruit.

All gathered together and stood in a ring
While the orange and purple around them did hang
They all whispered lowly and raised up their hands
Saying "Boys while you're living beware of the Bann."